The *Sweetest* Christmas Eve

Written by
Annie Hallinan

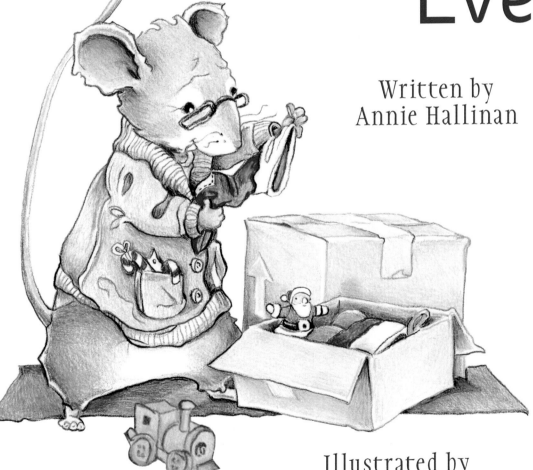

Illustrated by
Amy Preveza

A big thank-you to the Turnberry Advisory Team of Diane Adams, Betty Boyne, Judy Davis, Kelsey Envik, June Gardner, Julia Grubiak, Clare Leach, and Marie LoGiudice for their patient coaching.

A special heartfelt hug to Amy Preveza for her wonderful illustrations, Serena Kenyon-Brown for her "lovely" editing, and Judy Jones for her expertise with young readers.

In loving memory of Renee Robertson,

A.H.

Text copyright © 2023, 2016 Annie Hallinan

Jacket art and interior illustrations copyright © 2016 Amy Preveza

First printing: August 2016

Second printing: November 2023

Other works by Ms. Hallinan published by Turnberry Press:

> "Petrith Pin — The Wee Bear with the Big Difference" — 2017
>
> "Brinkley Boyd of Weymouth" — 2017
>
> "Haggis, Neaps and Tatties' Adventures in Scotland" — 2018

On page 2, the opening lines are from a poem by Clement Clarke Moore, "A Visit from St. Nicholas" (more commonly called "The Night Before Christmas"), published in the *Troy Sentinel,* Troy, New York, December 23, 1823.

Library of Congress Control Number: 2016937686

ISBN: 978-0-9971477-0-4

Published in the United States by:

Turnberry Press
145 Crest Road, Southern Pines, NC 28387 USA
www.TurnberryPress.com

Proudly printed in the United States of America

Turnberry Press

To Dusty, Bobby, Bettie, and Bob...

For all the wonderful Christmas Eves we shared together.

"T'was the night before Christmas
and all through the house,
not a creature was stirring,
not even a mouse."

Well, actually, that's not *quite* true...

Everyone was very active at Mouse Manor — after all,
it was Christmas Eve.

Mama Mouse was in the kitchen making dinner.

Papa Mouse was unpacking the boxes of Christmas stockings and ornaments; he was getting the house ready for Santa Mouse's visit that night.

The two little mice, Willie and Baby Zoie, were so excited. They simply couldn't sit still.

Giggling, they dashed from the kitchen to the family room and up the stairs to their bedroom.

And, then they did
it all again!

This was a special Christmas for the Mouse family. For a long time they had been living in some fairly shabby places and they frequently had to move. It seemed that every time they settled down, something would disrupt them.

The two little mice never knew when they would move or why. One time, Papa Mouse explained that it was because they were different from other folks, and people didn't always want a somebody different living so close to them.

Papa Mouse was very protective of his family. You see, mice are so tiny that everything is dangerous for them. Dogs and cats chase them, birds swoop them up for dinner, and snakes just want to gobble them up.

But people are the scariest of all.

People put mice in crates and carry them far away from their homes to cold, dark fields.

When you are a mouse, you understand quite early on that these things happen, and the best and only thing to do is to move to another place.

When they had moved and the little mice were safely asleep, Mama Mouse would cry.

But Papa Mouse would give her a big hug and tell her that things would be alright. Then he would sing to her and make her smile. He was such a lovely wee mouse.

However, many months ago, Papa Mouse had found the house where they lived now. Nobody lived nearby. Nobody bothered them. This year they would be celebrating the holidays in their very own home.

13

So it was wonderful that not only had Papa Mouse
found the most beautiful house in the entire world,
but also that they had lived there for many months.

That's a record length of stay in mouse history.

Mama Mouse had cried with happiness when she saw her new home. The little mice were startled because mums don't normally cry. They couldn't understand why the sweet new house made her weep. She had to explain to them that her tears were tears of joy and that her tears meant she was very happy.

This was
no ordinary
house; it was a
beautiful house. Every
room was full of
color with pink and
green and purple and yellow
walls. The fireplace had brown
bricks surrounded by shiny tiles, and
the Christmas tree lights made the tiles
sparkle.

Papa had to fix the walls when they crumbled a
bit; sometimes that happens in old houses.

All of their
mouse friends
came to visit. They
enjoyed Mama's tours
of the house. Being mice, they
especially enjoyed running up and
down the stairs. Mama Mouse
loved her house so much she simply couldn't
stop talking about it.

That made everyone chuckle.

But tonight was no time for worry. It was
Christmas Eve and everything seemed perfect.

Mama Mouse made an early dinner for Willie
and Zoie, knowing that they would
soon get sleepy.

And, so it was – the two little mice were
nodding off even as they tried to eat.

Mama carried them both upstairs, put them into their little beds and sang them a mouse fairy song. They smiled even as they yawned, because they had left cookies and milk for Santa Mouse.

As Mama finished tucking them into bed and turning off the lights, she smiled, too. She knew how excited they would be in the morning.

Papa also loved the house. But he was always a little bit scared they would have to leave their home when people discovered a mouse family living so close to them.

Papa Mouse took his tea and went to finish unpacking the Christmas boxes. Suddenly, he was spooked by a shadow.

He looked up and squealed: a woman was peering in the window!

She squealed at the same time as Papa Mouse. He tried to hide behind the cardboard boxes while the woman ran away, calling for someone.

Papa Mouse ran to tell Mama Mouse what had just happened.

As soon as she heard what he had seen, she was scared and sad. If a human sees you, you must leave quickly so that bad things don't happen to you and your family.

But Papa Mouse sat down on his chair. He was thinking so hard he had lines all over his forehead.

"Mama," he said, "What would you think if, instead of running away, we just stayed for a little while to see what will happen?"

Of course, Mama Mouse was alarmed. She sat down beside him and took his hand.

"This is our home, Papa, but people always make us leave, and I am worried about the safety of the little ones."

They both sat for a long time; at least, it seemed
to be a long time. Then Papa jumped up and
said, "This time is different, Mama. The
woman smiled after she shrieked.
I don't think she will do anything
bad to us. She had a kind
smile."

He was a very clever fellow,
and Mama trusted him.

They went up to Willie and Zoie's bedroom. Mama knew that if something happened, Papa had an escape plan. She put some things in her travel bag, in case they had to leave quickly.

They waited for a long time. Suddenly they heard footsteps. Papa peered out of the window and saw the woman and the man.

This was the moment that all mice dread — when people come to their home.

It always meant they had to run away, run away, run away fast.

But, to their amazement, the woman said, "Oh, Dan, it's Christmas. We bought this little gingerbread house so many years ago and we have always enjoyed it.

"Why don't we let the mice enjoy it just like we did?"

And that's what they did.

The man gently carried the gingerbread house and put it in an old shed at the back of the house. There the mice would be safe and warm, and would still live in their home.

The man hugged the woman, picked up Waffles the dog, and smiled. Then they went back into the big house.

The two little
mice heard the
commotion and
came running down
the stairs. They were
hoping Santa Mouse had
come. Papa told them about the
amazing visit from the two people.
Everybody agreed it was the best
Christmas gift, ever.

But Willie still wanted to know,
"Did Santa come?"

Christmas that year was truly very special. None of the Mouse family would ever forget the kindness of those people. The fact that little mice could live so close to humans and still be safe was a wonderful Christmas gift indeed.

Years later, when other mice say this story can't be true, Zoie smiles and tells them, "I was one of those little mice."

She lived in their sweet gingerbread house for a long, long time.

So, if
you have an old
gingerbread house,
check to see if a
wee mouse family
is living in it. Don't
be scared. Put out
a little cheese. And
let them have a very
Merry Christmas
eve.

Fairy Song from
"The Sweetest Christmas Eve"
Sing to: "Jingle Bells"

Fairy dust is magic
when sprinkled on a nose.
Makes a wee mouse sleepy,
right down to his toes.
So Mama sings a nice song
of how the fairies fly,
and how they tell all bad things
to go away - goodbye.

 Ohhh...Fairy dust, fairy dust, sprinkled on the nose
 Makes a wee mouse full of sleep, from his tail-tip to his toes

And then the fairies come,
in dreams as they would do,
so that little mice
would see them and smile too.
Cos' fairies are real special,
they make all things real bright,
They spread good cheer and magic dust,
then everything is right.
 Ohhh...

So go to sleep my babies,
don't fret about a thing.
The fairies and their magic dust
to you they sure will bring.
You'll wake up in the morning,
bright eyed and full of smiles,
With memories of cool toys and sweets
all stacked up in great piles.
 Ohhh...

Annie Hallinan

…is a long-time writer who grew up in Scotland. Her stories have an "old world" tone young readers enjoy. Writing stories for children has long been her passion, second only to rescuing abused animals. Critters and flowers are the focus of her stories. Annie lives in North Carolina with her husband and her three dogs.

Amy Preveza

…illustrated "The Sweetest Christmas Eve." Her hand-colored drawings gently move the reader into the tiny world of the Mouse family. She is married, a mother of three, and lives in Connecticut.

Turnberry Press